PIETY

PIETY

The Heartbeat of
Reformed Theology

JOEL R. BEEKE

PHILADELPHIA, PENNSYLVANIA

P&R
PUBLISHING
P.O. BOX 817 • PHILLIPSBURG • NEW JERSEY 08865-0817

Westminster Seminary Press, LLC, a Pennsylvania Limited Liability Company, is a wholly owned subsidiary of Westminster Theological Seminary.

This work is a co-publication between P&R Publishing and Westminster Seminary Press, LLC.

Scripture references are from the King James Version.

Italics within Scripture quotations indicate emphasis added.

ISBN: 978-1-59638-958-8 (pbk)
ISBN: 978-1-59638-959-5 (ePub)
ISBN: 978-1-59638-960-1 (Mobi)

Printed in the United States of America

Library of Congress Control Number: 2014936847

THE WORD *PIETY* has become a pejorative term today. Classifying someone as "pietistic" most often connotes excessive religiosity, self-righteousness, or a holier-than-thou attitude.

The etymology of the word *piety*, however, is more upbeat. The Old Testament term for this word means "the fear of the Lord," and its equivalent in the New Testament, *eusebia*, means "reverence for God" and "godliness." The Latin term for piety (*pietas*) indicates a childlike affection for God and his family. The German word (*fromm*) signifies "godly and devout" or "gentle, harmless, and simple." The English word implies pity and compassion.[1]

The sixteenth-century Reformers, most notably John Calvin (1509–64), would be shocked to see how poorly piety is regarded today, even among those who profess to be Reformed. For Calvin and his successors—the Protestant scholastics, the English Puritans, the Dutch Further Reformation divines, and, to some extent, the German Pietists—theology and practice were inseparably wed. Reformed theologians viewed piety as the heartbeat of their theology and of godly living.

Let us examine the importance of piety in Reformed theology, specifically in the work of Calvin, William Ames, and Gisbertus Voetius. We then will look at various definitions of Pietism, and conclude by offering some practical ways in which we may cultivate true piety in our daily lives.

1. This paragraph is adapted from Dale W. Brown, *Understanding Pietism* (Grand Rapids: Eerdmans, 1978), 9.

PIETY IN REFORMED THEOLOGY

John Calvin

Piety (*pietas*) is one of the major themes of Calvin's theology. While Calvin is known for his systematization of Reformed theology, his intellectual and doctrinal concerns must not be viewed apart from the spiritual and pastoral context in which he wrote his theology. As John T. McNeill rightly remarks, Calvin's theology is "his piety described at length."[2]

Calvin's concept of piety is rooted in the knowledge of God and includes attitudes and actions that are directed to the adoration and service of God. For Calvin, piety flows out of theology and includes heartfelt worship, saving faith, filial fear, prayerful submission, and reverential love.[3] Knowing who and what God is (theology proper) includes right attitudes toward God and doing what he wants (piety). Calvin connects theology and piety in his *Institutes of the Christian Religion*, stating, "I call 'piety' that reverence joined with love of God which the knowledge of his benefits induces."[4] According to Calvin, love and reverence for God are the necessary corollaries to true knowledge of him.

2. Quoted in John Hesselink, "The Development and Purpose of Calvin's Institutes," in *Articles on Calvin and Calvinism*, ed. Richard C. Gamble, vol. 4, *Influences upon Calvin and Discussion of the 1559 Institutes* (New York: Garland, 1992), 215–16.

3. Part of the first section of this essay has been adapted from Joel R. Beeke, "Calvin on Piety," in *The Cambridge Companion to John Calvin*, ed. Donald C. McKim (Cambridge: Cambridge University Press, 2004), 125–52, and from Joel R. Beeke, ed., *"The Soul of Life": The Piety of John Calvin* (Grand Rapids: Reformation Heritage Books, 2009). See also Lucien Joseph Richard, *The Spirituality of John Calvin* (Atlanta: John Knox Press, 1974), 100–101; Sou-Young Lee, "Calvin's Understanding of *Pietas*," in *Calvinus sincerioris religionis vindex*, eds. W. H. Neuser and B. G. Armstrong (Kirksville, MO: Sixteeenth Century Studies, 1997), 226–33; H. W. Simpson, "*Pietas* in the *Institutes* of Calvin," in *Our Reformational Tradition: A Rich Heritage and Lasting Vocation*, ed. T. Van der Walt (Potchefstroom, South Africa: Potchefstroom University for Christian Higher Education, 1984), 179–91.

4. John Calvin, *Institutes of the Christian Religion*, ed. John T. McNeill, trans. Ford Lewis Battles (Philadelphia: Westminster Press, 1960), 1.9 (hereafter *Inst.*).

Calvin says piety embraces every aspect of one's life. He writes, "The *whole* life of Christians ought to be a sort of practice of godliness."[5] This same concern for pious living is reflected in the subtitle of Calvin's first edition of the *Institutes*: "Embracing almost the whole sum of piety, & whatever is necessary to know of the doctrine of salvation: A work most worthy to be read by all persons zealous for piety."[6] Calvin's comments on 1 Timothy 4:7–8 also reflect the importance of *pietas*: "You will do the thing of greatest value, if with all your zeal and ability you devote yourself to godliness [*pietas*] alone. Godliness is the beginning, middle and end of Christian living. Where it is complete, there is nothing lacking. . . . Thus the conclusion is that we should concentrate exclusively on godliness, for when once we have attained to it, God requires no more of us."[7]

The supreme goal of this full-orbed piety is the glory of God. The primary desire of every regenerate person is to live according to the original purpose of creation—namely, that God may be glorified. Personal salvation, though critical, is therefore secondary for the pious person. So Calvin writes to Cardinal Sadolet:

5. *Inst.* 3.19.2 (italics added).

6. John Calvin, *Institutes of the Christian Religion: 1536 Edition*, trans. Ford Lewis Battles (Grand Rapids: Eerdmans, 1986). The original Latin title reads: *Christianae religionis institutio total fere pietatis summam et quidquid est in doctrina salutis cognitu necessarium complectens, omnibut pietatis studiosis lectu dignissimum opus ac recens editum* [*Joannis Calvini opera selecta*, eds. Peter Barth, Wilhelm Niesel, and Dora Scheuner, 5 vols. (Munich: C. Kaiser, 1926–52), 1:19 (hereafter *OS*)]. From 1539 on, the title was simply *Institutio Christianae religionis*, but "zeal for piety" continued to be a primary goal of Calvin's work. See Richard Muller, *The Unaccommodated Calvin: Studies in the Foundation of a Theological Tradition* (New York: Oxford University Press, 2000), 106–7.

7. *Calvin's New Testament Commentaries*, eds. David W. Torrance and Thomas F. Torrance, 12 vols. (Grand Rapids: Eerdmans, 1959–72), *The Second Epistle of Paul the Apostle to the Corinthians, and the Epistles to Timothy, Titus and Philemon*, trans. Thomas A. Smail (Grand Rapids: Eerdmans, 1964), 243–44 (hereafter, *Commentary* [on text]).

It is not very sound theology to confine a man's thought so much to himself, and not to set before him, as *the prime motive for his existence,* zeal to illustrate the glory of God. . . . I am persuaded that there is no man imbued with true piety who will not consider as insipid that long and labored exhortation to zeal for heavenly life, a zeal which keeps a man entirely devoted to himself and does not, even by one expression, arouse him to sanctify the name of God.[8]

The pious person's deepest concern is God: God's Word, God's authority, God's gospel, God's truth. Glorifying God—which is synonymous with pious living—means taking refuge in Jesus Christ for the forgiveness of sins and living within the bounds God has revealed.[9] The pious person's response to the gracious declaration of the gospel is complete surrender to the revealed will of God. In short, the comprehensive desire of the pious person is Calvin's oft-quoted vow: "I offer thee my heart, Lord, promptly and sincerely."

William Ames

William Ames (1576–1633), a renowned Puritan who authored a classic titled *The Marrow of Theology,* defines theology as "the doctrine or teaching [*doctrina*] of living to God."[10] For

8. *OS* 1:363–64 (emphasis added).

9. Calvin writes, "God has prescribed for us a way in which he will be glorified by us, namely, piety, which consists in the obedience of his Word. He that exceeds these bounds does not go about to honor God, but rather to dishonor him." *Ioannis Calvini opera quae supersunt omnia,* eds. Wilhelm Baum, Edward Cunitz, and Edward Reuss, *Corpus Reformatorum,* vols. 29–87 (Brunswick, Germany: C. A. Schwetschke and Son, 1863–1900), 49:51.

10. William Ames, *The Marrow of Theology,* trans. John D. Eusden (1629, 3rd ed.) (Boston: Pilgrim Press, 1968), 1.1.1. For the Latin, see Guilielmum Amesium, *Medulla s.s., theologiae: Ex sacris literis, earumque interpretibus, extracta, & methodice disposita per,* 4th ed. (London: Apud Robertum Allotium, 1630). For a biographical sketch

Ames, theology is a divine-human encounter that is not merely speculative but culminates in a practical end—the alignment of the human will with the will of a holy God.[11] In his fullest definition of theology, Ames concludes: "Theology, therefore, is to us the ultimate and the noblest of all exact teaching arts. It is a guide and master plan for our highest end, sent in a special manner from God, treating of divine things, tending towards God, and leading man to God. It may therefore not incorrectly be called θεοξία [*theoxia*], a living to God, or θεουργία [*theourgia*], a working towards God, as well as theology."[12]

Ames says that everything in the study of theology is related to practical godly living. He writes, "This practice of life is so perfectly reflected in theology that there is no precept of universal truth relevant to living well in domestic morality, political life, or lawmaking which does not rightly pertain to theology."[13]

Reformed theologians, such as Calvin and Ames, have always taught that godly living finds its source in God's gracious activity. According to Calvin, piety is rooted in the believer's mystical union (*unio mystica*) with Christ; this union is piety's starting point.[14] Union with Christ is possible because Jesus Christ assumed humanity, filling it with his virtue. Although Christ is not united with us in a crass mixture (*crassa mixtura*) of human

---

of William Ames and a summary of his classic, see Joel R. Beeke and Jan van Vliet, "*The Marrow of Theology* by William Ames," in *The Devoted Life: An Invitation to the Puritan Classics*, eds. Kelly M. Kapic and Randall C. Gleason (Downers Grove, IL: InterVarsity Press, 2004), 52–65. See also Jan van Vliet, "William Ames: Marrow of the Theology and Piety of the Reformed Tradition" (PhD diss., Westminster Theological Seminary, 2002). I am indebted to Jonathon Beeke for his assistance on this essay, particularly on this section about Ames.

11. Ames, *Marrow*, 1.1.9–13.
12. Ibid., 1.1.13.
13. Ibid., 1.1.12.
14. Howard G. Hageman, "Reformed Spirituality," in *Protestant Spiritual Traditions*, ed. Frank C. Senn (New York: Paulist Press, 1986), 61.

substances, nevertheless Calvin states, "Not only does he cleave to us by an indivisible bond of fellowship, but with a wonderful communion, day by day, he grows more and more into one body with us, until he becomes completely one with us."[15] This union, which is one of the gospel's greatest mysteries, is the fountain from which the pious, by faith, may draw for their sanctification.

Ames parallels this truth in his twofold division of theology. Owing to his Ramist predilection and its love of bifurcation, Ames believes theology can be divided into faith and observance.[16] The two are never separate, but their causal ordering can be distinguished. Ames, like Calvin, teaches that godly living flows from the benefits graciously given to those united to Christ. Theology's first act (*actus primus*) of faith—which Ames discusses in Book I of *The Marrow of Theology* and which includes union with Christ together with the double benefits received (justification and sanctification)—must not be divorced from theology's second act (*actus secundus*) of observance, taught in Book II, which includes good works, manner of worship, and love toward one's

---

15. *Inst.* 3.2.24.

16. For more on Ramism, see Walter Ong, who notes the inaccuracy of those who posit Ramus as a complete repudiation of anything Aristotelian. He writes, "Ramus' curricular reform program reveals the lines of battle drawn up between scholastic and humanist as well as the inability of either side to keep the lines completely firm. Recent close studies of Ramus have shown the tendentiousness and sheer ignorance of earlier interpretations which portrayed him as a nobly anti-Aristotelian humanist on a white charger scotching bloated scholastic dragons." In Ong's introduction to Peter Ramus, *Scholae in liberales artes*, vii, quoted in Gibbs's introduction to William Ames, *Technometry*, trans. Lee W. Gibbs (London: Milo Flescher, 1633; repr., Philadelphia: University of Pennsylvania Press, 1979), 71, n. 44. See also Richard Muller's helpful analysis of Ramist thought in his *Post-Reformation Reformed Dogmatics: The Rise and Development of Reformed Orthodoxy, ca. 1520 to ca. 1725* (Grand Rapids: Baker Academic, 1987), 1.4.1 (B.1) [hereafter *PRRD*], where he writes, "The seventeenth-century understanding of Ramism was, thus, not as a model that set aside Aristotle and scholastic method, but as model [*sic*] that modified and adapted both. Ramism emerges, therefore, not as an opposition to Protestant scholasticism but as a significant element in its framework and fashioning."

neighbor.[17] The justified and sanctified believer strives to be submissive to the will of God, to live to his glory, to acknowledge his supreme authority over all life, and to reverentially fear the Lord in *whole* obedience.

Gisbertus Voetius

Gisbertus Voetius (1589–1676), one of the greatest representatives of the Dutch Further Reformation (*Nadere Reformatie*), is a third model of Reformed piety.[18] Like Calvin and Ames, Voetius argued that piety and knowledge are not separate; rather, each promotes the other, for they are wedded. Voetius stressed this unity of piety and knowledge throughout his forty-two years as professor of theology at the Academy of Utrecht. In his inaugural address, *De pietate cum scientia conjugenda* ("On Piety Joined with Knowledge"), Voetius argued that the mind must assist the heart and life, and the heart and daily living must reinforce the mind. Like Ames, Voetius taught his students, "There is no part of your studies, which does not conduct the mind upwards, through the stages of creation, to higher things."[19] Battling against Cartesian rationalism, Voetius spoke against any attempt to weaken the link between knowledge and piety, saying that an absolute autonomy of science or knowledge is nothing other than unbridled libertinism. His objective at Utrecht was

17. See Richard A. Muller, *Dictionary of Latin and Greek Theological Terms: Drawn Principally from Protestant Scholastic Theology* (Grand Rapids: Baker, 1985), s.vv. "actus primus" and "in actu."

18. For a summary of the *Nadere Reformatie* and a discussion of the term, see Joel R. Beeke, *Assurance of Faith: Calvin, English Puritanism, and the Dutch Second Reformation* (New York: Peter Lang, 1991), 383–413. For a more complete overview of Voetian theology, see Joel R. Beeke, *Gisbertus Voetius: Toward a Reformed Marriage of Knowledge and Piety* (Grand Rapids: Reformation Heritage Books, 1999).

19. Gisbertus Voetius, *Ta asketika sive exercitia pietatis* (Gorinchem, Netherlands: Vink, 1654), 857.

to "practically treat the solid and orthodox science of theology, which is by nature practical."[20]

The writings of Voetius, along with his thirty-six years of pastoral work (including part-time preaching, visiting the sick, and catechizing Utrecht's orphan children), confirmed his love for the practice of theology (*theologia practica*), which induces God-glorifying piety. Though known for his polemics and scholastic methodology, Voetius was no ivory-tower theologian. Rather, he taught that the practical and experiential dimension of theology can be enhanced by the scholastic method, for, in the words of Johannes Hoornbeeck, "There is no practice without theory."[21] Like Ames before him, Voetius carefully distinguished theory and practice but never separated the two. A theology that is rooted in faith must be practical; it must, according to Voetius, be used to encourage the spiritual exercises of the divine graces of repentance, faith, hope, and love.

TWO FORMS OF PIETISM

Calvin, Ames, and Voetius all advocated a theology that encouraged holy, dependent living. They might therefore be called pietists. Some might recoil at that suggestion; however, I believe the term *pietist*, much like the term *puritan*, may be properly applied to more theologians than is sometimes done, provided we use the term *pietist*, with a lowercase *p*, rather than *Pietist*, with

20. Ibid., 3. For more on Voetius's refutation of Cartesianism, see Thomas A. McGahagan, "Cartesianism in the Netherlands, 1639–1676: The New Science and the Calvinist Counter-Reformation" (PhD diss., University of Pennsylvania, 1976); Theo Verbeek, "From 'Learned Ignorance' to Skepticism: Descartes and Calvinist Orthodoxy," in *Skepticism and Irreligion in the Seventeenth and Eighteenth Centuries*, eds. Richard H. Popkin and Ardo Vanderjagt (Leiden, Netherlands: E. J. Brill, 1993).
21. "Praxis nulla absque scientia est." See Johannes Hoornbeeck, *Theologiae practicae* (Utrecht, Netherlands: Versteegh, 1663), 1:85.

an uppercase *P*, which refers to members of the historical movement of Pietism that developed in Germany.[22] Let me explain. Defining pietism is not an easy task.[23] Comparing the historiographical development of this term to a "vast swamp," Carter Lindberg helpfully outlines two broad camps of "strict constructionist" and "transconfessional phenomenon."[24] The strict constructionists, led more recently by Johannes Wallmann, consider Pietism to be a definable historic movement that began in the late 1660s in Frankfurt, Germany, with a Lutheran pastor. Philipp Jakob Spener (1635–1705) became discouraged at the church's inability to motivate its parishioners to godly thinking and action, so he started meeting with small groups of believers on Sabbath afternoons to prompt Bible study and discussion. These groups, which Spener called *collegia pietatis* ("study classes in piety"), grew and spread throughout Germany and beyond. Critics of Spener dubbed those who belonged to these groups "Pietists." The movement lasted only a few generations, ending in the mid-eighteenth century, though its results have lingered until today.[25]

22. See F. Ernest Stoeffler, "Pietism: Its Message, Early Manifestation, and Significance," in *Contemporary Perspectives on Pietism: A Symposium*, ed. D. W. Dayton (Chicago: Covenant Press, 1976), 9–10. For a bibliography of German Pietism, see W. R. Ward, "Bibliographical Survey: German Pietism, 1670–1750," *Journal of Ecclesiastical History* 44 (July 1993): 476–505.

23. See Jonathan Strom, "Problems and Promises of Pietism Research," *Church History* 71 (September 2002), 536–54.

24. Carter Lindberg, introduction to *The Pietist Theologians: An Introduction to Theology in the Seventeenth and Eighteenth Centuries*, ed. Carter Lindberg (Oxford: Blackwell, 2005), 2–3.

25. See Johannes Wallmann, *Philipp Jakob Spener und die anfänge des Pietismus*, 2nd rev. ed. (Tübingen, Germany: Mohr, 1986); Wallmann, "Eine alternative geschichte des Pietismus: Zur gegenwärtigen diskussion um den Pietismusbegriff," *Pietismus und Neuzit* 28 (2002): 30–71. For a basic summary of Spener's life and piety, see K. James Stein, "Philipp Jakob Spener," in Lindberg, *The Pietist Theologians*, 84–99; for lengthier treatments, see Stein, *Philipp Jakob Spener: Pietist Patriarch* (Chicago: Covenant Press, 1986); and Dale W. Brown, "The Problem of Subjectivism in Pietism: A Redefinition with Special Reference to the Theology of Philipp Jakob Spener and

Wallmann asserts that Spener's contributions to Pietism (more specifically German Pietism) include a strong emphasis on Bible study, the use of small groups for spiritual fellowship (called the conventicle movement), the conviction that meeting in informal groups is a purer form of church than the organized church (i.e., the concept of the church within the church—*ecclesiola in ecclesia*),[26] and a strong eschatological hope for revival and "better times."[27] From Wallmann's perspective, a true definition of Pietism excludes kindred movements such as English Puritanism and the Dutch Further Reformation (*Nadere Reformatie*). He argues that including such movements negates Pietism as a verifiable historical movement and turns it into an "a-historical, typological concept."[28] Thus, Wallmann defines Pietism as the following:

August Hermann Francke" (PhD diss., Garrett Theological Seminary and Northwestern University, 1962).

26. Harry Yeide, *Studies in Classical Pietism: The Flowering of the Ecclesiola* (New York: Peter Lang, 1997).

27. Lindberg, *The Pietist Theologians*, 2. See also Manfred W. Kohl, "Spener's *Pia Desideria*: The Programmschrift of Pietism," in Dayton, *Contemporary Perspectives on Pietism*, 61–78.

28. Lindberg, *The Pietist Theologians*, 2. For a succinct summary of the similarities and differences between German Pietism, English Puritanism, and the *Nadere Reformatie*, see Joel R. Beeke, *The Quest for Full Assurance: The Legacy of Calvin and His Successors* (Edinburgh: Banner of Truth Trust, 1999), 288–93. See also Horst Weigelt, "Interpretations of Pietism in the Research of Contemporary German Church Historians," *Church History* 39 (1970): 236–41.

The roots of German Pietism have been variously designated. Heinrich Schmid believed it to be largely confined to the Lutheran church—*Die geschichte des Pietismus* (Nördlingen, Germany: Beck, 1863). Others viewed it as a renaissance of medieval mysticism—Albrecht Ritschl, *Geschichte des Pietismus*, 3 vols. (Bonn, Germany: Marcus, 1880); and Ronald R. Davis, *Anabaptism and Asceticism* (Scottdale, PA: Herald Press, 1974). Most scholars agree, however, that German Pietism has its roots in English Puritanism and/or the Dutch Further Reformation. Consult Heinrich Heppe, *Geshichte des Pietismus und der mystik in der Reformierten kirche, namentlich der Niederlande* (Leiden, Netherlands: E. J. Brill, 1879); August Lang, *Puritanismus und Piëtismus: Studies zu ihrer entwicklung von M. Butzer his zum methodismus* (Ansbach, Germany: Brugel, 1941); F. Ernest Stoeffler, *German Pietism during the Eighteenth Century* (Leiden, Netherlands:

Pietism arising in the seventeenth century and coming to full bloom in eighteenth-century continental European Protestantism as a *religious renewal movement* is, next to Anglo-Saxon Puritanism, the most significant religious movement of Protestantism since the Reformation. . . . Pietism pressed for the individualization and interiorization of the religious life, developed new forms of personal piety and communal life, led to sweeping reforms in theology and the church, and left profound marks on the social and cultural life of the countries grasped by it.[29]

Martin Brecht, on the other hand, does not limit pietism to the movement that began in Germany nor to the time frame of the mid-seventeenth to the mid-eighteenth century, but views pietism as a transconfessional phenomenon. Brecht says pietism began with Johann Arndt (1555–1621) and included English Puritanism, the Further Reformation of the Netherlands, and the more

---

E. J. Brill, 1973); Edgar C. McKenzie, "British Devotional Literature and the Rise of German Pietism," 2 vols. (PhD diss., St. Mary's College, University of St. Andrews, 1984); Peter Damrau, *The Reception of English Puritan Literature in Germany* (London: Many Publishing, 2006). Dale Brown provides a simple summary of this school of thought:

> By the age of fourteen Spener had read Lewis Bayly's *Praxis Pietatis* ("Practice of Piety") as well as other English Puritan devotional works by Dyke, Sonthom, and Baxter. Such Puritan literature, focusing on the conscience, the scrutinization of daily life, and the formulation of rules of living, was eagerly received in Pietist circles. Pietistic manifestations emerged in seventeenth-century Holland through Teellinck and his mysticism, Voet[ius] and his disciplined conventicles which spawned the movement called Precisianism, Koch [Cocceius] and his covenant biblical theology, Lodensteyn and his more charismatic conventicles, and Labadie (who had a profound influence on young Spener) and his radical and separatist tendencies. The impact of these Dutch reform activities spilled over onto German terrain, and historians have confirmed the similarity of the Dutch experience to what was to occur later in Germany by attaching the name Reformed Pietism to the movement. (*Understanding Pietism*, 17–18)

29. Wallmann, *Philipp Jakob Spener*, 7, quoted in Lindberg, *The Pietist Theologians*, 4.

radical Pietism of Germany.[30] Brecht, therefore, defines pietism as follows:

Pietism is the most significant devotional movement of Protestantism after the Reformation, and as such is primarily a religious phenomenon. Its spatial, temporal, social, spiritual, churchly-confessional, and theological range is simply astonishing and altogether constitutes its greatness as a historical subject. Pietism arose around the turn of the sixteenth to the seventeenth century from criticism of the existing ecclesiastical and spiritual relations at nearly the same time in England, the Netherlands, and Germany, spreading from there to Switzerland, Scandinavia, Eastern Europe, and the United States. It contributed to a great extent to the world-wide Protestant mission, and has remained a living movement into the present.[31]

I would advocate, then, that pietism (lowercase, as advocated by Brecht) is the broader category, whereas Pietism (uppercase, as advocated by Wallmann) best describes the movement that is sometimes called German Pietism. With this distinction in mind, both the concerns of Wallmann and Brecht are satisfied; pietism denotes the wider connectivity that Brecht espouses, whereas Pietism denotes the narrower discontinuity that Wallmann emphasizes.[32]

In *The Rise of Evangelical Pietism*, F. Ernest Stoeffler, much like Brecht, argues that the "experiential element within all Ref-

30. See Martin Brecht, "Pietismus," in *Theologische realenzyklopädie*, eds. Gerhard Krause and Gerhard Müller (Berlin: de Gruyter, 1996), 26: 606–31.

31. Martin Brecht, et al., eds., *Geschichte des Pietismus* (Göttingen, Germany: Vandenhoeck & Ruprecht, 1993), 1:1, quoted in Lindberg, *The Pietist Theologians*, 4.

32. Another possible solution, advocated by Dale Brown, is to use *Pietism* exclusively for the movement that originated in the German context, and then apply adjectives to describe other cousin movements, such as *Reformed Pietism* to designate English Puritanism and the Dutch Further Reformation (*Understanding Pietism*, 16). The weakness of this approach is that scholars are not always agreed on what these adjectives should be.

ormation churches of the seventeenth and eighteenth centuries should be seen in its essential oneness."[33] Stoeffler asserts that this element of pietism, whether in England, Scotland, Russia, Denmark, or North America, and whether linked to Calvinistic, Lutheran, or Arminian theology, is *one* historic entity. Stoeffler thus says: "It is the conviction that all experiential Protestantism during the post-Reformation period can be treated as an essential unity. It constitutes a movement which, if seen in its full range, penetrated all of Protestantism during the seventeenth and eighteenth centuries and the influence of which has been felt wherever Protestantism has appeared."[34] Yet, in emphasizing the connectivity in all forms of experiential Protestantism, Stoeffler fails to distinguish adequately between Pietism and pietism. Moreover, if Reformed piety is an experiential response to Reformed theology, it is impossible for Arminian piety, for example, to be identified with Reformed piety.

Stoeffler provides a fascinating list of marks that help identify pietism in its broader sense.[35] (I have added more to his list for the sake of comprehensiveness.) The marks of pietism include: (1) increasing emphasis on Bible study, (2) engaging frequently and at length in fervent prayer, (3) exercising spiritual fellowship through conventicles, (4) using the Bible as a

---

33. F. Ernest Stoeffler, *The Rise of Evangelical Pietism*, Studies in the History of Religions 9 (Leiden, Netherlands: E. J. Brill, 1971), 7. Elsewhere Stoeffler provides the following marks as the major distinctives of German Pietism: (1) radical inward renewal, (2) the practice of piety (*praxis pietatis*), (3) religious fellowship called *koinonia*, (4) the "oppositive element"—i.e., the idea that most in the church are still children of the world and true Christians must form a contrary lifestyle, (5) the inseparableness of love for God and for man, (6) spiritual illumination, and (7) Christian growth ("Pietism: Its Message, Early Manifestation, and Significance," in Dayton, *Contemporary Perspectives on Pietism*, 10–14).

34. Ibid., 8.

35. Ibid., 3–18.

textbook for godly living, (5) experiencing the presence and reality of Christ in daily events, (6) emphasizing continuing repentance, (7) cultivating an inward devotional life through daily devotions and the means of grace, (8) singing psalms, (9) engaging in evangelism and mission outreach, (10) monitoring and highlighting the Lord's Supper, (11) minimizing the differences between clergy and laity, and promoting greater lay participation in nearly every aspect of religious activity, (12) obeying the Decalogue out of gratitude to God, (13) experiencing joy in the Lord (felicity), (14) encouraging Word-focused and soul-saving preaching, (15) accenting the invisible church more than the visible, (16) stressing cross bearing and personal sacrifice, (17) focusing on the primary purpose of theology, which is living in the presence of God (*coram Deo*) to God's glory, (18) tending to accent a rather dramatic conversion, (19) maintaining family worship, (20) catechizing the laity, (21) stressing personal and corporate spiritual revival,[36] (22) publishing edifying literature, (23) stressing theological education for clergy, (24) keeping the Sabbath by dedicating the entire day to God, (25) advocating the priesthood of all believers, (26) stressing works of mercy, (27) demonstrating biblical stewardship so all of life is surrendered to God, (28) meditating on biblical truths and duties, and (29) keeping spiritual diaries.[37]

While related, Pietism and pietism are not identical because of their various emphases. Both Spener and August Hermann Francke (1663–1727),[38] the fathers of Pietism, shifted the focus

---

36. For a study on revival movements within German Pietism, see Howard Albert Snyder, "Pietism, Moravianism, and Methodism as Renewal Movements: A Comparative and Thematic Study" (PhD diss., University of Notre Dame, 1983).

37. For an explanation of many of these marks, see Brown, *Understanding Pietism*.

38. For a basic summary of Francke's life and piety, see Markus Matthias, "August Hermann Francke," in Lindberg, *The Pietist Theologians*, 100–114.

from the theoretical to the practical nature of pietism more than the English Puritan ministers did.[39] For example, Francke, who was an administrative genius, worked hard to translate Spener's agenda into action by founding institutions to propagate it. Gottfried Arnold (1666–1714) established the Orphan House (1695) at Halle, which became a focal point for Pietism, much as the University of Halle became in the next century.[40] Pietism emphasized the "inner person," limiting the role of the public ministry of the church and promoting the personal reading and discussion of Scripture in smaller devotional gatherings.[41] Under the influence of Spener and Francke, Pietism more formally proposed "the interiorizing of faith, individual experience, the directing of justification toward the 'new creature' and the fruits of rebirth."[42] In some cases, the Pietism of the seventeenth and eighteenth centuries evolved into separatist, anthropocentric (as opposed to theocentric) religion; in other cases, however, Pietists remained active in society.

We should not assume that the major concerns of German Pietism were foreign to Reformed theology in Britain, the Netherlands, and elsewhere. Surely Reformed theologians did not overlook Pietism's application of redemption and its effects in the lives of believers, as was made evident in our review of the theological systems of Calvin, Ames, and Voetius. Godly living is the end goal of Reformed theology. So the theology of the Reformers and their successors (Protestant orthodoxy) is not adverse to piety; rather, as Richard Muller has ably demonstrated, many of the Lutheran

39. See Gordon Stevens Wakefield, *Puritan Devotion: Its Place in the Development of Christian Piety* (London: Epworth Press, 1957).

40. Phyllis Tickle, foreword to *The Pietists: Selected Writings*, eds. Emilie Griffin and Peter C. Erb (San Francisco: Harper, 2006), vii.

41. Lindberg, *The Pietist Theologians*, 8.

42. Ibid.

and Reformed orthodox, if they are to be measured against the Pietist theologians, "could match Spener in warmth of piety."[43]

What, then, is the difference between the pietism of Reformed theology and the Pietism of Spener and Francke? As I have stressed earlier, true piety rests on the foundation of right teaching. Stated more technically, the objective faith that is believed (*fides quae creditor*) provides the contextual basis for the subjective faith by which one believes (*fides qua creditor*); the latter must accept the confession of the former.[44] Lionel Greve thus says all piety "demonstrates the interdependence between piety and theology. The specific response of man to God is determined by theology. Hence, we might say that piety has objective and subjective dimensions. Theology gives piety its objective content."[45] Only in this manner can doctrinal confession and piety coexist; it is this proper and causal relationship that the Pietist theologians failed to stress to the same degree as the English Puritans and most Dutch Further Reformation divines. Piety expressed in this manner does not become anthropocentric. It does not slide into a legalistic religion of works but finds its source (*principia*) in the objective accomplishment of redemption in Jesus Christ.

Confusing misconceptions arise when the word *Pietism* (uppercase) is used to describe English Puritanism or the Dutch Further Reformation, for these terms represent distinct movements that differ in important areas. For example, many Ger-

---

43. Muller, *PRRD*, 2.2.2 (B.3). See also Ted A. Campbell, *The Religion of the Heart: A Study of European Religious Life in the Seventeenth and Eighteenth Centuries* (Columbia: University of South Carolina Press, 1991).

44. See Muller, *PRRD*, 1.1.2 (A.1).

45. Lionel Greve, "Freedom and Discipline in the Theology of John Calvin, William Perkins and John Wesley: An Examination of the Origin and Nature of Pietism" (PhD diss., Hartford Seminary Foundation, 1975), 273.

man Pietists spoke out against doctrinal precision, showing, as Jonathan Gerstner says, "a marked antipathy for all but the most simple doctrinal concepts."[46] This was a marked contrast to Calvin, English Puritans such as Ames, and Dutch Further Reformation leaders such as Voetius, who consistently sought to merge theology and piety. Then too, German Pietism developed some practices that were less prominent in Puritanism and the Dutch movement, such as singing Christ-centered hymns, reaching out socially through orphanages, and accenting ecumenical ideals.

In summary, German Pietism, English Puritanism, and the Dutch Further Reformation had much in common. Each was rooted in the sixteenth-century Reformation, and each longed for more thorough reform. Each had a pietistic flavor and pietistic practices. Each movement was imbued with pietism. Yet each movement had a distinct historical, theological, and spiritual character. Each movement began within its respective churches, but, over time, developed as a distinctive phenomenon, partly because of the reactions of authorities and different groups in society. Despite similar forms of religious experience and piety, each developed into a complex, religious, and social movement that spanned all classes of society.[47]

46. Jonathan Neil Gerstner, *The Thousand Generation Covenant: Dutch Reformed Covenant Theology and Group Identity in Colonial South Africa, 1651–1814* (Leiden, Netherlands: E. J. Brill, 1991), 76. See also Egon W. Gerdes, "Theological Tenets in Pietism," in Dayton, *Contemporary Perspectives on Pietism*, 25–60.

47. Willem van't Spijker, "De Nadere Reformatie," in *De Nadere Reformatie: Beschrijving van haar voornaamste vertegenwoordigers*, ed. W. van't Spijker (The Hague, Netherlands: Boekencentrum, 1986), 5–16. See also Van't Spijker, *De Nadere Reformatie en het Gereformeerd Piëtisme* (The Hague: Boekencentrum, 1989); Hartmut Lehmann, "The Cultural Importance of the Pious Middle Classes in Seventeenth-Century Protestant Society," in *Religion and Society in Early Modern Europe 1500–1800*, ed. Kaspar von Greyertz (London: Allen & Unwin, 1984), 33–41.

Over the centuries, these groups influenced religious and intellectual Western culture,[48] particularly North American conservative Reformed and Presbyterian churches and seminaries.[49] Consider how many of the twenty-nine marks of pietism are still prevalent today, particularly in churches that stress the necessity of Reformed experiential preaching and the need to marry theology and godly living into a seamless whole as the believer strives to live to God's glory. Dale Brown says the continuing legacy of pietism is evident today in our emphasis on the personal, the experiential, the ethical, and the necessary change of heart.[50] All those who might be called pietists stress that true Christianity involves experiencing a personal, meaningful relationship with God. Consequently, pietists stress personal repentance and faith, warm devotion, the obedience and assurance of faith, and an experiential acquaintance with God. Such beliefs usually result in a strong emphasis on discriminatory preaching, personal conversion, and evangelistic outreach. Pietists have always stressed the need for vibrant faith, which strives to persuade complacent church members and unbelievers to

48. See Marilyn J. Westerkamp, *The Triumph of the Laity: Scots-Irish Piety and the Great Awakening, 1625–1760* (Oxford: Oxford University Press, 1988).

49. See Joseph Haroutunian, *Piety Versus Moralism: The Passing of the New England Theology* (New York: Henry Holt, 1932); John Rodney Fulcher, "Puritan Piety in Early New England" (PhD diss., Princeton University, 1963); Michael McGiffert, ed., *God's Plot: The Paradoxes of Puritan Piety* (Boston: University of Massachusetts Press, 1972); Gerald Francis Moran, "The Puritan Saint: Religious Experience, Church Membership, and Piety in Connecticut, 1636–1776" (PhD diss., Rutgers University, 1973); F. Ernest Stoeffler, ed., *Continental Pietism and Early American Christianity* (Grand Rapids: Eerdmans, 1976); Glenn T. Miller, *Piety and Profession: American Protestant Theological Education, 1870–1970* (Grand Rapids: Eerdmans, 2007).

50. Dale W. Brown, "The Continuing Legacy of Pietism Today," in Dayton, *Contemporary Perspectives on Pietism*, 75–89; also Brown, "A Contemporary Critique," in *Understanding Pietism*, 137–64.

repent of their sin, believe in Christ alone for salvation, and commit themselves to obedient faith and godly piety in every sphere of their lives.

MEANS THAT CULTIVATE PIETY

Having examined the influence of piety in Reformed theology, as well as some examples of its misapplication, let us now propose the means by which godly living may be cultivated. The Reformed have continually stressed the means of grace to promote growth in piety. Thus, let us demonstrate the relationship between the means of grace and piety, specifically focusing on the Holy Spirit's connection with piety through the church and through private spiritual disciplines.

Piety Cultivated by the Church

Though some segments of German Pietism have downplayed this, most genuine piety is nurtured by the believer's connection with the church established by Jesus Christ. Piety is not simply individualistic but has a predominant ecclesiological dimension. Believers are engrafted into Christ *and* his church, and spiritual growth occurs *within* the church. The visible church, as Calvin teaches, is therefore the mother, educator, and nourisher of every believer, for the Holy Spirit acts in her according to his promises.[51] Believers cultivate piety by the Spirit through the church's worship and teaching ministry, progressing

51. *Inst.* 4.1.1. Calvin writes, "For there is no other way to enter into life unless this mother [the *visible* church] conceive us in her womb, give us birth, nourish us at her breast, and lastly, unless she keeps us under her care and guidance until, putting off mortal flesh, we become like the angels" (*Inst.* 4.1.4). See also Joel R. Beeke, "Glorious Things of Thee Are Spoken: The Doctrine of the Church," in *Onward, Christian Soldiers: Protestants Affirm the Church*, ed. Don Kistler (Morgan, PA: Soli Deo Gloria, 1999), 23–25.

from spiritual infancy to adolescence to full maturity in Christ; they do not graduate from the church on earth until they die.[52]

The believer's life is therefore a lifelong education of piety within the church community. Because the believer is united to Christ as Head of his church, it is impossible to progress in piety apart from the church. The pietists taught that there are four important means by which we grow in piety through the church:

The Preached Word. Growth in piety is integrally connected to the preached Word of God. A holy God comes down to meet us, address us, and make himself known to us in his Word, especially in its preached form, to which godly piety responds with adoration, prayer, love, submission, and trust. Through the preaching of the gospel, the Spirit works faith and repentance, enabling the believer to respond in piety. As Calvin says, it is by the Spirit-empowered preaching of men that "the renewal of the saints is accomplished; thus the body of Christ is built-up."[53] Furthermore, the preached Word of God is the divinely appointed instrument for the healing, cleansing, and making fruitful of disease-prone souls.[54] The "external minister," who is the ordained preacher, is employed by the "internal minister," who is the Holy Spirit. The minister is like a doctor who can diagnose and offer the remedy for spiritual maladies in people plagued by sin and death. Those remedies are then applied profitably to souls by the Holy Spirit. In short, the revelatory Word of God, most fully expressed in Jesus Christ, is the source of the believer's new life of obedient and thankful submission.

52. *Inst.* 4.1.4–5.

53. *Inst.* 4.3.2. See also *Inst.* 4.1.5; *Commentary* on 1 Cor. 13:12.

54. John Calvin, *Sermons of M. John Calvin, on the Epistles of S. Paule to Timothie and Titus,* trans. L. T. (1579; repr. facsimile, Edinburgh: Banner of Truth Trust, 1983), on 1 Tim. 1:8–11.

Pietism teaches that we should make diligent use of the preached Word. The Puritans in particular relished good sermons. They attended church faithfully, took careful notes, and often talked and prayed their way through the sermon afterward with their children. These practices were the fruit of Puritan pastors teaching their people how to listen to sermons. Here is a digest of Thomas Watson's advice:

1. Prepare to hear the Word by bathing your soul in prayer.
2. Come to the Word with a holy appetite and a tender, teachable heart.
3. Be attentive to the preached Word.
4. Receive with meekness the engrafted Word (James 1:21).
5. Mingle the preached Word with faith.
6. Strive to retain what has been preached and pray about the Word proclaimed.
7. Put the Word into practice; be doers of it.
8. Beg the Spirit to accompany the Word with effectual blessing.
9. Familiarize yourself with the Word by sharing it with others.[55]

The Sacraments. Much like the Word of God, the sacraments of holy baptism and the Lord's Supper are God's gifts to his people in which he accommodates himself to our weakness in order to encourage, edify, and nourish us. Calvin links growth in piety to the sacraments, defining them as testimonies "of divine grace toward us, confirmed by an outward sign, with mutual attestation

55. Thomas Watson, *Heaven Taken by Storm*, ed. Joel R. Beeke (Morgan, PA: Soli Deo Gloria, 1992), 16–18; and Watson, *A Body of Divinity* (London: Banner of Truth Trust, 1971), 377–79.

of our piety toward him."[56] The sacraments are thus "exercises in piety" that foster and strengthen our faith, and encourage us to offer ourselves as living sacrifices to God. Baptism, which signifies and seals the believer's washed state in the blood of Jesus Christ, encourages the believer to live a Spirit-renewed life as an adopted child of the heavenly Father.[57] Likewise, the Lord's Supper signifies and seals the believer's union with the crucified and risen Savior, demonstrating that new life comes only by partaking of Christ.[58] When we meet Christ in the sacraments, we grow in grace, which is why they are called means of grace. The sacraments promote confidence in God's promises through Christ's redemptive death. They encourage us in our progressive life of piety toward heaven.

We should make diligent use of the sacraments, the pietists said, since they spur us to Christlikeness and therefore to piety. Grace received through the sacraments is similar to that received through the Word. Both convey Christ. But as Robert Bruce writes, "While we do not get a better Christ in the sacraments than we do in the Word, there are times when we get Christ better."[59]

The Communion of Saints. We should seek fellowship in the church, the pietists said. It is wise to spend time with mentors in holiness (1 Cor. 11:1; Eph. 4:12–13).[60] The church ought to be a fellowship of mutual caring and a community of prayer (Acts 2:42; 1 Cor. 12:7). We should talk to and pray with fellow believers

56. *Inst.* 4.14.1.

57. See Ronald S. Wallace, *Calvin's Doctrine of the Word and Sacrament* (London: Oliver & Boyd, 1953), 175–83; H. O. Old, *The Shaping of the Reformed Baptismal Rite in the Sixteenth Century* (Grand Rapids: Eerdmans, 1992).

58. See Brian A. Gerrish, "Calvin's Eucharistic Piety," in *The Legacy of John Calvin,* ed. David Foxgrover (Grand Rapids: CRC, 2000), 53.

59. Robert Bruce, *The Mystery of the Lord's Supper,* trans. and ed. Thomas F. Torrance (Richmond, VA: John Knox Press, 1958), 82.

60. See Belgic Confession of Faith, Art. 28.

whose godly walks we admire (Col. 3:16). And we should heed Proverbs 13:20, which says, "He that walketh with wise men shall be wise." Watson said that association promotes assimilation.[61] A Christian life lived in isolation from other believers will be defective and spiritually immature. We cannot have a *heavenly* fellowship if we promote a *hindering* fellowship.

Piety, then, is much fuller than a simplistic "me and Jesus" or "me and my Bible" approach. Contrary to the many misinterpretations of piety, Reformed theology teaches that it is fostered within the context of a community of saints. Within the church, believers "cleave to each other in the mutual distribution of gifts."[62] Each covenant member is given gifts to be used in collective harmony and symmetry, keeping all members of the community reforming and growing in holiness and devotion.[63]

The Exercise of Church Discipline. Piety is further promoted through the spiritual discipline of the church, which is closely linked to the means of grace.[64] Unconditional obedience to God's revealed will is the essence of piety, for love, freedom, and discipline are all connected. Piety includes rules that govern the believer's response, both privately and publicly. In both cases, the glory of God compels disciplined obedience in following Christ.

---

61. Thomas Watson, *A Body of Practical Divinity* (Edinburgh: Banner of Truth, 1983), 87, 249.

62. *Commentary* on 1 Cor. 12:12.

63. *Commentary* on 1 Cor. 4:7.

64. See especially Belgic Confession of Faith, Art. 32, which reads: "Therefore we admit only of that which tends to nourish and preserve concord and unity, and to keep all men in obedience to God. For this purpose excommunication or church discipline is requisite, with the several circumstances belonging to it, according to the Word of God." Art. 29 defines discipline as a third mark of the church, along with the preaching of "the pure doctrine of the gospel" and "the pure administration of the sacraments as instituted by Christ."

Publicly, piety is expressed in the exercise of church discipline. We must not see church discipline as a form of legalistic service that demands complete renunciation of this world and extreme forms of asceticism and mysticism. Rather, the discipline exercised by office bearers in Christ's church is medicinal; it encourages Christians to live a life of holy, responsive, and gratuitous obedience to God. Discipline practiced in this manner offers the law, not as a set of rules one must follow to be counted worthy, but as guidelines whereby the Christian may express gratitude for being counted worthy in Christ. Piety is not a legalistic observance of the law but a life of love conversant with the law that flows from one's standing in Christ. Piety is not an isolationist form of spirituality but a lifestyle of loving both God and neighbor sincerely and actively. Spiritual discipline promotes this type of living. In true piety, the freedom of love and the discipline of obedience coalesce.

From these considerations, we may conclude that piety is primarily cultivated within the context of the church. The preaching of the gospel, the administration of the sacraments, the communion of saints, and the spiritual discipline of the church work together to promote godly living in the home, the church, the school, and the marketplace.

Piety Cultivated by Private Disciplines

Privately, the guidelines and rules of discipline are also critical for developing personal piety. These rules include exercising the fear of God, daily repentance, neighborly love, self-denial, cross bearing, and, in general, living as obedient strangers and pilgrims in this life with one eye always on eternity. All of these important graces of the Christian life tend to be strengthened through private spiritual disciplines, which, in turn, assist us as members of Christ's church to grow in genuine piety.

Since the Puritan pietists excelled in this area, let me provide the kind of practical advice they gave for developing piety through private spiritual disciplines. These private disciplines include:

Reading and Searching the Scriptures. If you would grow in sanctification, the Puritans advised, read through the Bible diligently at least once a year. Also, take time to study the Word. Absorb it into your soul by comparing Scripture with Scripture (John 5:39). Absorbing God's Word is the primary road to holiness and to spiritual growth. Peter advised, "Desire the sincere milk of the word, that ye may grow thereby" (1 Peter 2:2).

Do not expect to grow in holiness if you spend little time alone with God and do not take his Word seriously. Richard Greenham asserts that we should read our Bibles with more diligence than men dig for treasure. He says diligence makes rough places plain, the difficult easy, and the unsavory tasty.[65]

When you are tempted to wander from the King's highway of holiness, let Scripture teach you how to live a holy life in an unholy world. Follow the advice of Henry Smith: "We should set the Word of God always before us like a rule, and believe nothing but that which it teacheth, love nothing but that which it prescribeth, hate nothing but that which it forbiddeth, do nothing but that which it commandeth."[66] If we do these things, we will concur with the Puritans, who attested that the Scriptures teach us "the best way

65. Richard Greenham, *The Works of the Reverend and Faithfvll Servant of Iesvs Christ, M. Richard Greenham,* ed. H[enry] H[olland] (London: Felix Kingston for Robert Dexter, 1599), 390.
66. Henry Smith, *The Works of Henry Smith* (Edinburgh: James Nichol, 1860), 1:494.

of living, the noblest way of suffering, and the most comfortable way of dying."[67]

Meditating on the Scriptures. After reading Scripture, we must meditate on it (Ps. 1:2). Reading offers knowledge, but meditation and study add depth to that knowledge. The difference between reading and meditation is like the difference between drifting in a boat and rowing toward a destination.

The Puritans spoke often of meditating on God's Word. Thomas Hooker defines the art of meditation as "a serious intention of the mind, whereby we come to search out the truth and settle it effectually upon the heart."[68] He and other Puritans suggest the following ways to meditate on Scripture:

1. Pray for the power to harness your mind—to focus by faith on the task of meditation.
2. Read the Scriptures, then select a verse or two or a doctrine on which to meditate.[69]
3. Memorize verse(s) to stimulate meditation, to strengthen faith, to help you witness and counsel others, and to serve as a means of divine guidance.
4. Meditate on what you know about your verse(s) or subject, probing the book of Scripture, the book of conscience, and the book of nature.[70] As you meditate, think of applications

67. Benjamin Keach, *Preaching from the Types and Metaphors of the Bible* (Grand Rapids: Kregel, 1972), xvii.

68. Thomas Hooker, *The Application of Redemption by the Effectual Work of the Word and Spirit of Christ, for the Bringing Home of Lost Sinners to God* (London: Peter Cole, 1659), 2:210.

69. For a list of profitable subjects for meditation, see *The Works of Stephen Charnock* (Edinburgh: James Nichol, 1865), 3:307.

70. *The Works of George Swinnock* (Edinburgh: Banner of Truth Trust, 1998), 2:417.

to your own life. "Take every word as spoken to yourselves," Watson writes.[71]

5. Stir up affections, such as love, desire, hope, zeal, and joy, to glorify God.[72]

6. Arouse your mind to some duty and holy resolution.[73]

7. Conclude with prayer, thanksgiving, and psalm singing. Psalm singing has been a great boon for private devotions for believers who have engaged in it.[74]

Praying and Working. Prayer and work (*ora et labora*) belong together. They are like two oars that, when used together, keep a rowboat moving forward. If you use only one oar—praying without working or working without praying—you will row in circles.

Piety and prayer are closely related because prayer is the primary means of maintaining communion with God. Here are five important guidelines the Puritans offer about praying:

1. Give priority to prayer. Prayer is the first and most important thing you are called to do. "You can do more than pray

---

71. Thomas Watson, "How We May Read the Scriptures with Most Spiritual Profit," in *Heaven Taken by Storm*, 122.

72. Richard Baxter, *The Saints' Everlasting Rest* (Ross-shire, UK: Christian Focus, 1998), 579–90; and Jonathan Edwards, *The Religious Affections* (London: Banner of Truth Trust, 1959), 24.

73. William Bates, *The Works of the Rev. W. Bates D.D.* (Harrisonburg, VA: Sprinkle, 1990), 3:145; and Thomas White, *A Method and Instructions for the Art of Divine Meditation* (London: Tho. Parkhurst, 1672), 53.

74. See Joel R. Beeke and Ray B. Lanning, "The Transforming Power of Scripture," in *Sola Scriptura: The Protestant Position on the Bible*, ed. Don Kistler, 2nd ed. (Orlando: Reformation Trust, 2009), 131–33. For a fuller treatment of Puritan meditation, see Nathanael Ranew, *Solitude Improved by Divine Meditation, or A Treatise Proving the Duty, and Demonstrating the Necessity, Excellency, Usefulness, Natures, Kinds, and Requisites of Divine Meditation* (Morgan, PA: Soli Deo Gloria, 1995); Simon Chan, "The Puritan Meditative Tradition, 1599–1691: A Study in Asceticality" (PhD diss., Cambridge University, 1986); and Joel R. Beeke, *Puritan Reformed Spirituality* (Darlington, England: Evangelical Press, 2006), 73–100.

after you have prayed, but you cannot do more than pray until you have prayed," John Bunyan writes. "Pray often, for prayer is a shield to the soul, a sacrifice to God, and a scourge to Satan."[75]

2. Give yourself—not just your time—to prayer. Remember that prayer is not an appendix to your life and your work, it is your life—your real, spiritual life—and your work. Prayer is the thermometer of your soul.

3. Give room to prayer. The Puritans did this in three ways. First, they had real prayer closets—rooms or small spaces where they habitually met with God. When one of Thomas Shepard's parishioners showed him a floor plan of the new house he hoped to build, Shepard noticed that there was no prayer room and lamented that homes without prayer rooms would be the downfall of the church and society. Second, block out stated times for prayer in your daily life. The Puritans did this every morning and evening. Third, between those stated times of prayer, commit yourself to pray in response to the least impulse to do so. That will help you develop the "habit" of praying so that you will pray your way through the day without ceasing. Remember that conversing with God through Christ is our most effective way of bringing glory to God and of having a ready antidote to ward off all kinds of spiritual diseases.

4. Give the Word to prayer. The way to pray, said the Puritans, is to bring God his own Word. That can be done in two ways. First, pray *with* Scripture. God is tender of his own handwriting.[76] Take his promises, turn them inside out,

75. John Bunyan, "Dying Sayings" in *The Works of John Bunyan*, ed. George Offor (1854, repr. Edinburgh: Banner of Truth, 1991), 1:65.

76. *The Complete Works of Thomas Manton* (London: James Nisbet, 1872), 6:242.

and send them back up to God by prayer, pleading with him to do as he has said. Second, pray *through* Scripture. Pray over each thought in a specific Scripture verse.

5. Give theocentricity to prayer. Pour out your heart to your heavenly Father. Plead on the basis of Christ's intercessions. Plead to God with the groanings of the Holy Spirit (Rom. 8:26). Recognize that true prayer is a gift of the Father, who gives it through the Son and works it within you by the Spirit, who, in turn, enables it to ascend back to the Son, who sanctifies it and presents it acceptable to the Father. Prayer is thus a theocentric chain, if you will—moving from the Father through the Son by the Spirit back to the Son and the Father.

Genuine piety calls for well-planned, hard, and sweat-inducing prayer and work, the Puritans said. Careful planning as to how you are going to live for the Lord is necessary if you want to achieve much of abiding value for him. Yet the Puritans were not self-reliant. They understood that daily living for a Christian must go something like this:

1. Look ahead and see what you have to do.
2. Go to the Lord in prayer and say, "Lord, I do not have what it takes to do this; I need divine help."
3. Rely on the Lord to answer the prayer you have offered, then proceed expectantly to the task that lies before you.
4. After completing the task, return to the Lord to thank him for the help he gave.
5. Ask his forgiveness for all your failures and sins in the process, and ask for grace to fulfill your task more faithfully the next time.

The Puritan method of daily piety includes earnest prayer and hard work without self-reliance; all the exertion of energy is done in faith. By grace, exercising piety is both faithful effort and fruitful effort.

Journaling. The Puritans viewed journaling or diary keeping as an optional means of grace that can greatly benefit believers in cultivating piety. Journaling can help us express thoughts to God and to ourselves that otherwise remain buried. It can assist us in meditating and praying, in remembering the Lord's works and faithfulness, in understanding and evaluating ourselves, in monitoring our goals and priorities, and in maintaining other spiritual disciplines.[77]

Reading Spiritually Edifying Literature. Puritan ministers frequently published their sermons in books. According to Alan F. Herr: "The printing of sermons constituted a rather large business in Elizabethan England. It has been estimated that more than forty per cent of all publications issued at that time were religious or philosophical in nature and it is evident that sermons account for a large part of those religious publications."[78] In the last three decades of the sixteenth century alone, more than three hundred volumes of Puritan sermons were published in England.[79] More recently, more than 90 percent of the seven hundred Puritan books reprinted since the beginning of the resurgence of Puritan literature in the late 1950s consist of revised sermons.[80]

77. For a good summary of Puritan-like thinking here, see Donald S. Whitney, *Spiritual Disciplines for the Christian Life* (Colorado Springs: NavPress, 1991), 196–210.
78. Alan F. Herr, *The Elizabethan Sermon* (New York: Octagon Books, 1969), 67.
79. Ibid., 27.
80. For a listing and brief reviews of all of these titles, see Joel R. Beeke and Randall Pederson, *Meet the Puritans* (Grand Rapids: Reformation Heritage Books, 2006).

Throughout the centuries, Reformed pietists have promoted such reading as an important means for promoting holiness. Dutch pietists, for example, fondly called the Further Reformation authors the "old writers" (*oude schrijvers*) and were greatly nourished spiritually by their books.

THEOLOGY AND PIETY: NECESSARY COROLLARIES

At its heart, Reformed theology is pietistic; the concern of Reformational theology is as practical as it is doctrinal. As the majority of the orthodox divines affirm, theology is partly theoretical, partly practical (*partim partim*);[81] the head and heart are necessary corollaries of each other. For Calvin and his successors, the Reformation included the reform of piety (*pietas*), or spirituality, as much as a reform of theology. The spirituality that was cloistered behind monastery walls for many centuries reduced piety to celibate, ascetic, and penitential devotion. Reformed theologians, however, helped Christians to understand that true spirituality flows from its principal source, Jesus Christ. The Christian's actions in the family, field, workshop, and marketplace—in short, the entire scope of life—are to be a grateful, pious reflection of the grace found in Jesus Christ.

This dual emphasis of nurturing both the mind and the soul is sorely needed today. On the one hand, we confront the problem of dry Reformed orthodoxy, which correctly teaches doctrine but lacks emphasis on vibrant, godly living. The result is that people

81. For a representation of the *partim partim* construction, see Johannes Wollebius, *Compendium theologiae Christianae* (Basel, 1626), translated by Alexander Ross as *The Abridgment of Christian Divinity*, 3rd ed. (London: T. Mabb for Joseph Nevill, 1660), 1.29.10, where he wrote, "Faith that is not united to firm trust, is no better than historical faith. The papists teach that faith is only in the intellect, not in the will and the heart. Scripture expressly declares the contrary: 'With the heart man believes unto justification' (Rom 10:10)."

bow before the doctrine of God without yearning for a vital, spiritual union with the God of doctrine. On the other hand, Pentecostal and charismatic Christians often propose emotionalism in protesting a formal, lifeless Christianity, but this emotionalism is not solidly rooted in Scripture. The result is that people put human feeling before the triune God as he reveals himself in Scripture. The genius of genuine Reformed piety is that it marries theology and piety so that head, heart, and hand motivate one another to live for God's glory and our neighbor's well-being. Greve summarizes piety well when he concludes:

> Piety, then, is a quality of Christian life expressed by obedience in fear and love, law and grace, command and promise. Understood in this manner, piety [has] an ecumenical quality. It recognizes no denominational loyalties. . . . It can be maintained in the world as well as in the Church. Its charter is the Bible and [its] goal, the glory of God. It is not a static quality of life but a dynamic one. [It is] a quality of Christian life that is in a state of dynamic tension—continuously hovering between freedom and discipline. It is founded in fear, yet is manifested in love. It demands the rigorous use of law, yet is lived in grace. It requires obedience but voluntary obedience. The glory of God is its goal, yet all mankind benefits from its presence. True piety cannot be confined behind institutional walls. Its very structuring destroys it. Yet it is and was found in institutions. . . . The very nature of the Church demands piety.[82]

Piety understood in this sense is not something to be despised or shunned; rather, we are called to promote it in the Reformation teaching of holy, dependent, loving, and godly living. Being called

82. Greve, "Freedom and Discipline," 284.

"pious" or "pietistic" in its true sense is a compliment! If we think otherwise, we need to reconsider our definition of piety. Does our definition stem from its proper use in Scripture or from its improper application in radical Pietism and in much of contemporary society? Godliness, spirituality, or piety is not a means to an end (i.e., eternal, felicitous life), but an expression of this end merited by Jesus Christ. For this reason, the cultivation of piety is preeminently connected to the means of grace. In short, piety means experiencing sanctification as a divine, gracious work of renewal expressed in repentance and righteousness, which progresses through conflict and adversity in a Christlike manner for all of a believer's life, anticipating the day when piety will be perfected in eternal sanctification in heaven.